MONSTER TRUCKS

MORE THAN

100

MONSTROUS PHOTOS!

MICHAEL BENSON

EDITOR

RANDOM HOUSE VALUE PUBLISHING, INC.
NEW YORK • AVENEL, NEW JERSEY

For Antonia Jasmine Pocock

The editor wishes to thank the following persons and organizations,
without whose help the creation of this book would have been impossible:
Mike Bargo, Nancy Davis, Rita Eisenstein, Richard Gilbert,
Paul Hallasy, David Hutchison, David Henry Jacobs, Kurt Kleinau,
Jean Krevor, Milburn Smith, United States Hot Rod Association,
and all the folks who build and drive these beautiful monsters.

Copyright 1994 © Michael Benson

All rights reserved.

Library of Congress Cataloging-in-Publication Data

Monster trucks / edited by Michael Benson.
      p.   cm.
   Includes index.
   ISBN 0-517-11974-9 :
   1. Monster trucks.   I. Benson, Michael.
TL230.5.M68M66   1994
796.7—dc20 `   94-16233
                       CIP

All photos, unless otherwise noted, are © Starlog Communications International, Inc., by Mike Bargo.

Printed and bound in China

© Starlog Communications International, Inc., by Scott W. Aszkenas.

*Perhaps you've wondered what happens when a monster truck
gets a five-and-a-half-foot flat tire. Well . . .*

TABLE OF CONTENTS

FOREWORD

MONSTER TRUCK MANIFESTO

by David Henry Jacobs

Here's a list, in no particular order, of ten reasons why monster trucks are good for you, our nation, and the world:

1. **PATRIOTISM**. Monster truck fans are patriotic. Everybody was on their feet when ''The Star Spangled Banner'' was played before the start of the big monster truck extravaganza at the New Jersey Meadowlands this year. Not a single soul remained seated—which is a better average than you'd find on a college campus, or a baseball game.

2. **INVENTIVENESS**. Science and technology combine to bring you the cutting edge of automotive excitement. First came monster trucks, then mud boggers, monster trax, Beastron, and the World's Largest Transformer. I can't wait to see what they'll think of next, can you?

3. **BIGNESS**. Americans love bigness, and monster trucks are an expression of our national mania for giantism.

4. **STYLE**. They look great. Even the names sound sharp: Bounty Hunter, Liquidator, Rocky Mountain Thunder, Excaliber, etc.

5. **THRILLS**. Monster truck drivers defy gravity to bring you the best in daredevil excitement.

6. **POWER**. Monster truck drivers embody raw power. Breathes there a man with soul so dead, that he never wanted to climb behind the wheel of a monster truck?

7. **POTENTIAL**. Monster trucks haven't been around that long, and look at the big fun they've already generated. And this is only the beginning.

8. **CYBORGERY**. Monster trucks are helping pave the way for the coming of the Cyborg, the ultimate man-machine fusion.

9. **AMERICANISM**. The covered wagon, Colt revolver, clipper ship, television, and Mom's apple pie are all unique expressions of the American spirit. Monster trucks, likewise.

10. **UNIVERSAL APPEAL**. North of Alaska and South of the Border, East of the Rising Sun and West of the Moon, folks around the world love those monster trucks.

Now, editor Michael Benson, world's greatest automotive photographer Mike Bargo, and the gang at Starlog's MONSTER TRUCK SPECTACULAR magazine bring you all of the mammoth mobile thrills that can be packed into one book! Join the crusade, as monster trucks conquer the world!

David Henry Jacobs is the Associate Editor of the Starlog Publications WAR PLANES OF THE MIDDLE EAST and AMERICA AT WAR.

INTRODUCTION

FANTASY GRIDLOCK BUSTERS

by Michael Benson

It has happened to you. You're on the road in your car or truck and you're in a hurry to get someplace. Then you stop in a traffic jam and you sit, and sit, and sit, and sit.

Maybe there was an accident up ahead. Maybe the big football game just let out, and clogged up a major traffic artery. Whatever it is, the road you're on has just turned into one long parking lot!

The driver of the car in front of you just got out to stretch and the driver behind you thinks he can make everyone disappear if he only honks his horn long enough.

Your life suddenly feels like sand in a sieve—and you think:

"If I were driving a monster truck right now, I'd..."

You'd crush, that's what you'd do! You'd throw her into gear and drive right over the cars in front of you!

Maybe that's the primary appeal of monster trucks: They are the ultimate in fantasy gridlock busters!

So we hope you enjoy the 40 fantastic trucks on the following pages. Our recommendation is: Let your fantasies run wild!

Michael Benson is the editor of MONSTER TRUCK SPECTACULAR and STOCK CAR SPECTACULAR magazines. He has authored four books, VINTAGE SCIENCE FICTION FILMS, BALLPARKS OF NORTH AMERICA, DREAM TEAMS and WHO'S WHO IN THE JFK ASSASSINATION.

How does an object
this heavy fly? Power, that's how!

FIRST BLOOD

LEAPS SIX CARS, NO SWEAT!

Rob Fuchs' "First Blood" Ford monster is widely respected as one of the best performing trucks—and for good reason: it can leap over six (and sometimes more) cars on any given day, and rarely breaks anything in his suspension or axles.

Few trucks can take the constant punishment that Fuchs gives his truck. His secret is in the suspension, as you'll find out later in this chapter.

Like just about every other monster-truck driver/owner, Fuchs got into the monster truck field for the thrill and excitement of performing in a truck he built himself.

Fuchs, a resident of Woodstock, Illinois, started building monster trucks in 1988, when he built the original First Blood truck. During his first summer of performing, he took it out to crush cars at the Great Lakes Dragaway, a past proving ground for such trucks as Bear Foot, the original King Kong, Goliath, Kodiak and many others.

Owner/driver Ron
Fuchs gives First Blood the "once over" before a recent live performance.

Popularity Grows

The crowds immediately went crazy for Fuchs' truck. After running some of the bugs out of it, he began crushing cars for big-time promoters like Standing Room Only (SRO,) American Truck Puller and Main Attraction Promotions.

These promoters sent Fuchs all across the country. As his popularity grew, the truck demanded more of his time. His day-job boss—Fuchs worked as an engineer for a brake-parts manufacturer—was kind enough to allow him a leave of absence so that he could take his truck on the road.

Soon he was so busy, and successful, at running First Blood that he decided to make it his full-time profession—and today, maintaining the First Blood monster remains his obsession.

This is a job that would be more than full time for any person. The truck needs constant attention. Even when it's running perfectly there is always some gravel that kicks up and dings the paint job, or a hydraulic line that leaks, or something else that needs time for fixing.

First Blood is an exceptional car-crusher because of its low center of gravity and the front springs, which allow the front tires to give when they hit cars.

Lower Center of Gravity

First Blood has the body of a customized Ford F350. The sheet metal was donated to Fuchs by Suburban Ford of Woodstock, and its stunning DuPont "scarlet red" acrylic lacquer was painted by Friedel Auto Body in the same town.

To the basic body, Fuchs has added a double-white roll bar, KC lights and chrome bumpers. The interior is stock, with the exception of the tachometer and engine temperature gauges.

The suspension has a lower center of gravity than that of most other monster trucks and is designed to "give" when it hits cars. This means the front springs recoil backwards when the front tires hit cars. The long front struts are also hydraulic, allowing them to recoil on impact.

Whatever bends doesn't break, so this flexibility in the front end greatly enhances the durability of the parts. The suspension was designed and built by Len Manning of Spring Align in Palatine, Illinois. Manning also built First Blood's fuel system.

Under the Hood

The power Fuchs needs to launch over cars comes from First Blood's Dyer blown Ford 466 motor, bored .030 over, with a Crower cam, two Predator carburetors, custom ported 429 Cobra jet heads, Arias pistons, aluminum rods, and Hedman headers.

Dyer, the number-one Midwestern maker of blowers, is located on the south side of Chicago, Illinois and is close enough to give Fuchs technical assistance and parts for the blower whenever he needs them.

With this engine, Fuchs figures he gets at least 700 horsepower and 750 pounds per foot of torque at 5500 rpm. This power is routed via a Ford C-6 automatic transmission to a two-and-a-half-ton military transfer case, then down to the five-ton Rockwell military axles and their Clark planetary ends.

The planetary gears are not standard on the military axles. They are made by cutting off the old hubs and welding on the

*First Blood's Dyer blown Ford 466
under the hood gives it the power it needs
to launch over six or more cars on any given night.*

hubs from Clark axles. To keep the truck sleek, Fuchs narrowed it a bit, cutting a little more off the axles before welding on the new hubs.

The final gear ratio of the drive train is 20:1, about the same as other monsters. Engine power is kept on both rear tires by a Detroit locker differential.

The huge Goodyear Terra tires, 66 inches tall, are used on First Blood. Their immense weight is controlled by Monroe 70 shock absorbers. There are three shocks on each front wheel, where they are needed to dampen the impact of hitting cars, and two on each rear wheel.

All told, Fuchs spent about a year and a half on the truck, $80,000 for parts and $30,000 for labor. Doug Harland, who has his own sleek monster truck named "Over Excited," was indispensable in the building of First Blood, and Harland still helps out with the maintenance of the truck.

MONSTER FACTS

Name: First Blood
Owner: Rob Fuchs, Woodstock, Illinois
Vehicle: Ford F350 Custom
Engine: Ford 466
Aspiration: Two Predator carburetors
Horsepower: 700 @ 5500 rpm
Transmision: Ford C-6 automatic
Transfer Case: Rockwell two-and-a-half-ton military
Axles: Rockwell five-ton military
Differentials: Detroit locker
Hubs: Clark planetary
Ring & Pinion: 6.44:1
Wheels: FTC steel 36 x 25
Tires: 66-inch Goodyear Terra
Paint: DuPont scarlet red acrylic lacquer
Height: 126 inches
Width: 136 inches
Length: 178 inches
Cost to build: $110,000

WORLD'S LARGEST TRANSFORMER

CAR-EATING MONSTER!

At first sight this monster truck looks like a 1950s monster movie come alive—it has moving hands, arms and jaws, and seems to attack cars as it lifts them up and crushes them in its mouth!

This Hollywood-like creation is no illusion: it's a real 20-ton car-munching machine that has thrilled monster truck fanatics all over the United States. The creature is called the World's Largest Transformer and it transforms itself out of an army tank.

It is owned by International Promotions, Inc. of Chandler, Arizona. Stanley Torgerson, who runs International Promotions, came up with the concept for this transformer. He worked with fabricators to have the creature built. Construction took more than a year.

The World's Largest Transformer isn't just a giant car-crunching dinosaur. It actually is a transforming vehicle.

Picture This . . .

The box-like tank pulls up in front of a crowd, and the top opens. Then, the green arms and claws of the creature slowly emerge from the top, followed by the head.

The creature unfolds out of the vehicle to become a three-story-tall mechanical dinosaur, complete with arms, claws, head and jaws. The eyes light up and then—you have to see it to believe it—smoke comes out the nostrils and it breathes fire like Godzilla!

The World's Largest Transformer is based on an ordinary M4 Personnel Carrier, like the ones used in monster tanks.

The transformer's hydraulic system gives it its power. The power for the hydraulic system—which makes the monster move its arms, claws and jaws—is provided by a shaft that is connected to the engine's driveshaft.

There are 800 feet of hydraulic hose in the transformer, and the hydraulic pump can move more than 30 gallons of hydraulic fluid per minute at 2,500 psi.

Tummy rumbling with hunger, the creature then approaches a junk car and takes a big bite out of the sheet metal! The World's Largest Transformer does this several times and then blows flames on the car. The car catches on fire and the crowd roars with astonishment!

After the car is torn up and ablaze, the creature throws it to the ground and looks for another one.

The Secret: Hydraulics

No one who sees the World's Largest Transformer has seen anything like it before. It's one thing to see a gigantic monster in a movie, the impressive result of stop-motion trick photography or rear-projection techniques—but it's a completely different matter when you can actually feel the ground rumble as the 41,000-pound monster approaches and feel the heat of the flame as it starts cars on fire.

The transformer accomplishes these feats with a lot of sophisticated, powerful, expensive technology. It is based on an ordinary M4 Personnel Carrier, like the ones used in monster tanks.

It has a 427-cubic-inch Chevrolet engine that was removed from a drag car and re-cammed for high torque.

The transformer's hydraulic system gives it its power. The power for the hydraulic system—which makes the monster move its arms, claws and jaws—is provided by a shaft that is connected to the engine's driveshaft.

There are 800 feet of hydraulic hose in the transformer, and the hydraulic pump can move more than 30 gallons of hydraulic fluid per minute at 2,500 psi. The transformer's arms are 14 feet long, and with this hydraulic system, can generate 50,000 pounds of lifting power!

The jaws have more than 15,000 pounds of biting force, and can bite objects as large as six feet in diameter. This means that,

The transformer's arms are 14 feet long, and with this hydraulic system, can generate 50,000 pounds of lifting power!

The jaws have more than 15,000 pounds of biting force, and can bite objects as large as six feet in diameter.

when performing at shows, the World's Largest Transformer can lift an old Buick or Cadillac (weighing three tons or more) and bite right through the doors, trunk, roof and sides.

It's easy for the transformer to pick up cars, since each hand has more than 10,000 pounds of crushing force!

And It's Fast Too!

Not only can this transformer pick up cars and crush them, put cars in its mouth and chew them, or blast them into blazes with its fiery halitosis, but it can also rumble right over the top of cars, crushing them as it goes, at a speedy 40 miles per hour.

Stanley Torgerson says it cost "a lot of money" to build the World's Largest Transformer—but, he adds, "It was worth it." Fans who are in awe whenever they see this beast perform can't help but agree.

We've seen monster trucks that were loud, big, strong, powerful and fast—but this is the first time we ever saw one that was HUNGRY!

It has a 427-cubic-inch Chevrolet engine that was removed from a drag car and re-cammed for high torque.

It took more than a year to build the transformer, but fans from coast-to-coast agree that it was worth it!

The Godzilla-like transformer is owned by International Promotions, Inc. of Chandler, Arizona.

BEASTRON!

The first monster tank—a monster truck set on tank tracks—was conceived and built by Willie Townes of Virginia Beach, Virginia. Townes' next creation was a monster robot, Beastron!

Beastron is set on tank tracks, much like the tracks used by other monster tanks, but this monster also transforms into a space age robot who shoots fire, "tosses" bombs and offers some good advice to the crowd.

According to Beastron's story, he is actually a visitor from another planet, who was sent here on a mission to warn Earth kids about the dangers of taking drugs.

To demonstrate the seriousness of his message, Beastron shoots flames out of his hands and appears to throw bombs that blow up monster-flattened junk cars. He knows how to get a kid's attention!

One thing that a monster-truck show isn't is quiet, so it is unusual when the yet-to-be-transformed Beastron tank first rolls out in front of a crowd, because it does so with hardly a sound.

Then the space-age robot slowly rises out of the tank vehicle—and rises, and rises . . . The robot doesn't stop growing until he reaches his full height of 20 feet. His head turns from side to side. His arms move up and down.

Then the flames start shooting, the bombs start going off and Beastron begins his inspirational speech.

Beastron is rather unassuming, and almost completely silent, before it starts to morph. These photos were taken during a Beastron performance at Broadway Bob's Great Lakes Dragaway in Union Grove, Wisconsin. Builder Willie Townes has to act like a puppeteer to control the movements of his robot.

Ordinary Chevy Engine

Beastron is built on a set of M4 tank retriever tracks and uses an ordinary Chevrolet engine for power. It has some high-performance components in the engine and is capable of producing approximately 500 horsepower.

The effect of fire coming from Beastron's hands is achieved by propelling propane gas through electrical sparks. The feat is particularly stunning when Beastron performs at night. The robot is 100% safe and has never had a mishap. And Beastron can also drive over and crush cars, just like "regular" monster trucks do! Beastron has some high-performance components in the engine and produces about 500 horsepower.

The arms, body and head are hydraulically powered, using 360 feet of hydraulic hose. The hydraulic pump is powered by the Chevy engine. The fire comes from 40-pound propane tanks ignited by electric sparks, while the explosives are placed on the junk cars ahead of time and then exploded by remote control during the show.

Townes says that he did not have a lot of experience with hydraulics when he built Beastron.

"I overbuilt it," he comments.

The arms, for example, are two-inch hydraulic cylinders, which are powerful enough to lift up a small car. Townes uses the strength in those arms to his advantage, however. Beastron has been known to lift heavy objects during shows.

Beastron can also drive over and flatten cars, just like other monster trucks do, but the other stunts it does are much more difficult. Townes has to act like a puppeteer during a show. He synchronizes the movements of the tank, head, arms and body, just as if he were pulling the strings on a marionette. Instead of pulling strings, however, Townes controls Beastron with hydraulic switches.

100% Safe

Beastron is 100% safe for shows, and has never had a mishap. In fact, the only time Beastron ever suffered damage was when Townes was driving through Pennsylvania and hit a wet spot on the road.

He slid off the highway and Beastron rolled off his trailer. The fins and other body parts on one side were damaged.

Townes merely picked Beastron up, put him back on his trailer, fixed him and drove him 3000 miles to the state of Washington, where Beastron didn't miss a single performance.

Townes and his robot monster can be seen all over the country performing to the thrill of children and adults alike. Beastron frequently performs through the auspices of the United Sports of America promotional group.

HEARTLAND EXPRESS!

THE BEAST FROM BREWTOWN!

The Heartland Express is the beautiful creation of Guy and Debbie Wood of Milwaukee, Wisconsin. It's obvious that the Woods have put great care into this beast's construction and paint job—and the Heartland Express has plenty of oomph beneath the hood to boot!

The truck's power source is a 468-cubic-inch Chevrolet engine, custom-made with 13:1 pistons, $^7/_{16}$ rods, a forged crankshaft, square port head that's been ported and polished, titanium valves, Holley 950 carburetor and zoomie headers.

Heartland Express's drivetain consists of a TCI high-performance turbo 400 transmission, a two-and-a-half-ton military transfer case that feeds both front and rear axles for four-wheel drive, and 30-ton Pettibone axles taken from heavy

equipment. To keep the truck perched up over the huge 66-inch-tall Goodyear Terra tires, the Woods have a set of custom-built front springs with 12 inches of arch, and 18 inches in the rear pair, dampened by 18 Rugged Trail shock absorbers.

Beautiful Body

The body of Heartland Express features many customized accessories, such as a Westin double-tube roll bar, a 14-inch drop bumper in the rear, a Warn front bumper, a Pro Net tail-gate net, and six KC Daylighter lights.

The body has been painted a striking combination of candy-apple red, blue and silver by Top Gun Paint and Body Specialists—with the lines of trim by Beanpole.

The interior features a custom overhead console, dual sunroofs, rear sliding window, custom seat, blue carpeting—and gauges for oil, engine temperature, engine rpm, and amps.

The Woods would like to point out that Heartland Express could never have been their dream-come-true without the assistance of the Kodiak Off-Road Center, Kim's Engine Service and National Spring.

Heartland Express has a set of custom-built front springs with 12 inches of arch, and 18 inches in the rear pair, dampened by 18 Rugged Trail shock absorbers.

When Heartland Express hits the row of cars it becomes an angry beast, rearing up on its hind legs, er, wheels. This monster is nicknamed the "Brewtown Beast" because it was conceived and born in Milwaukee, Wisconsin.

The body has been painted a striking combination of candy-apple red, blue, and silver by Top Gun Paint and Body Specialists—with the lines of trim by Beanpole.

EXCALIBER!

Racing monster trucks are built with a different philosophy than the true behemoths of the field. The bigger-the-better way of thinking that guided the early years of monster truck action has given way—at least partially—to the faster-the-better philosophy that came when racing was introduced to the sport. Now state-of-the-art racing monsters have gone hi-tech, with computers designing their suspensions.

Sounds pretty modern, right? Well, Dave Marquart and Mike Nickell have been using computer technology to design their monster suspensions ever since they designed and built the original Excaliber—several generations before the model you see here—back in 1985. (That original was a 1985 Chevy pickup, and was used until it rolled over and the body was crushed.)

The Computer Aided Design (CAD) system enables the designers to "fit" all the parts together on the computer first, without having to worry about clearances for the driveshaft, space for the shocks, etc.

The wheels are held to the ground—and under the truck—by a custom-made suspension that uses custom-made springs (made by Toledo Spring) with 12 inches of wheel travel. These are kept under control by Trail Master N7 gas shock absorbers.

Excaliber's powerplant is a Chevrolet 454 bored to 468 cubic inches. It also has a Blower Drive Service (BDS) supercharger with 38% overdrive. The fact that it's fuel-injected on alcohol greatly increases the horsepower.

The entire monster truck can be designed from the ground up on the computer, then actually assembled later after the designers know how everything is going to fit together.

38% Overdrive

The current Excaliber, shown here, has the power to compete with the best racing monsters in the world. It has raced on television during the Camel Mud & Monster Series.

Excaliber's powerplant is a Chevrolet 454 bored to 468 cubic inches. It also has a Blower Drive Service (BDS) supercharger with 38% overdrive. The fact that it's fuel-injected on alcohol greatly increases the horsepower.

The cylinder heads are also ported and polished, and the engine breathes with custom-made, hand-built headers. Now Excaliber has 1,250 horsepower, enough to rocket its relatively heavy 13,800 pounds into the air. But don't let its weight fool you. It's a very competitive truck. The computer has seen to that.

The drivetrain consists of a lightweight aluminum Pro Fab transfer case, turbo 400 automatic-racing transmission built to high-performance specifications, and five-ton Rockwell axles with Clark planetaries in the ends. These carry the big Firestone 66-inch tires and FTC wheels.

The wheels are held to the ground—and under the truck—by a custom-made suspension that uses springs (made by Toledo Spring) with 12 inches of wheel travel. These are kept under control by Trail Master N7 gas shock absorbers. The frame was custom made by Marquart and Nickell, using the stock frame reinforced by rectangular tubing at stress points.

The interior features a custom Mastercraft driver's seat. This is a racing-quality seat that is custom made to fit perfectly to the contours of the driver's back, who is usually Marquart.

Other safety features include a full list of Monster Truck Racing Association (MTRA) safety items, such as a roll cage, an engine shutoff, an ignition kill switch and u-joint shrouds. This Excaliber has taken its computer technology from coast-to-coast, touring the country for the United States Hot Rod Association.

HEARTBEAT!

Brett Engelmann has been around the monster-truck circuit for a long time. He once drove the awesome Michigan Ice Monster. Now he drives a truck called Heartbeat.

The truck has undergone some changes since Engelmann first started using it to crush cars into pancakes. Some of the changes were intentional. Some of them weren't. But, whatever the cause, all of the changes have been for the good, as you can see from the way this beast performs.

Heartbeat has an awesome 431-cubic-inch Chevrolet engine that is supercharged and injected with alcohol. This gives the truck a heart-stopping 1,400 horsepower, enough to send it rocketing over the highest pile of cars.

13,500 Pounds of Monster

Heartbeat has an awesome 431-cubic-inch Chevrolet engine that is supercharged and injected with alcohol. This gives the truck a heart-stopping 1,400 horsepower, enough to send it rocketing over the highest pile of cars.

Hooked up to the engine are a turbo 400 transmission, a two-and-a-half-ton airshift military transfer case and 20-ton Clark planetary axles. To keep the hefty 13,500-pound mon-

ster under control, Engelmann uses custom-made leaf springs and 12 Trail Master shock absorbers.

The huge five-and-a-half-foot-tall Goodyear Terra tires also cushion the shock of car crushing. Between the engine and

Those of you who saw the original Heartbeat monster truck might remember that it was black. But all of the sheet metal had to be changed when Engelmann rolled it over during a show at Arrowhead Stadium in Kansas City. Engelmann had the truck up and running in a mere ten days, and when Heartbeat made its comeback appearance its new signature colors were white, pink, and blue.

suspension, Engelmann's Heartbeat was a top contender during the Camel Mud & Monster series.

Heartbeat has been stripped down to the sheet metal to save weight. The inside door panels have been removed, there is no carpeting, and there is only one custom-racing seat (for the driver.)

Heartbeat has toured the country for several major promoters, including the United States Hot Rod Association, Standing Room Only and United Sports of America.

Safety First

Brett Engelmann is aware of the safety necessary in motorsports competition, and has Heartbeat fully equipped with all MTRA safety items. These include:

- built-in roll cage
- fire extinguisher
- ignition kill switch
- fuel cell
- safety harness
- racing seat
- provision for remote control engine shutoff

Aside from these safety items and a few gauges, the interior of Heartbeat is stock!

4-WHEEL CRAZY!

BUILT FOR SPEED!

Rob Morris of Fort Worth, Texas was an unknown in the monster-truck circuit when he built his truck called 4-Wheel Crazy, based on a Ford Ranger Supercab body.

But Morris didn't stay unknown for long. In his first year of competition, 4-Wheel Crazy proved to be one of the four fastest monster trucks in the world.

Morris might have been unknown in the world of monsters, but he was well known indeed as a maker of customized trucks, being the owner of a shop called "4-Wheel Technology" near Fort Worth.

To make his Ford Ranger as quick as it is, Morris used a 461-cubic-inch engine with a GMC 671 supercharger with 30% overdrive, fed with injected alcohol.

Morris figures his powerplant produces

To make his Ford Ranger as quick as it is, owner/builder Rob Morris used a 461-cubic-inch engine with a GMC 671 supercharger with 30% overdrive, fed with injected alcohol.

approximately 1,000 horsepower. Since the truck weighs 12,500 pounds—light for the old days, but on the heavy side today—Morris has enough power for now, but hopes to lighten 4-Wheel Crazy in the near future.

The engine is plumbed with stainless-steel braided hoses and fitting from Russell Performance. Chromed Hooker zoomie headers help it breathe. The engine was worked on by International Automotive Machine of Fort Worth—and its output is routed through an Art Carr turbo 400 transfer case, using an Art Carr torque converter with a 3,500 rpm stall speed.

The power is directed to the two driveshafts via a two-and-a-half-ton military airshift transfer case, then custom-made driveshafts (fabricated by Texas U-Joints) route the power to the Rockwell axles.

The axles have Clark planetary gears in the hubs for extra strength. Running 1,000 horsepower through a 12,500-pound truck requires an awful lot of extra strength in the axles!

These axles turn the big, heavy, 66-inch-tall Firestone tires that are mounted to custom-made steel wheels, 25 by 36 inches in size. The tires and the frame are held together through the suspension, which is made of Super Lift modified leaf springs and 16 Rugged Trail shock absorbers, the 60,000 Series size.

To support the body over these heavy axles, Morris has a custom-made frame, fabricated out of boxed C-channel steel and ⅜-inch steel plate. This provides greater stiffness and carrying capacity to the frame, while the steel plates are used to mount the shocks and oversize leaf springs. The body of 4-Wheel Crazy is kept in condition through the help of South Town Ford in Fort Worth, and Quinton & Sons Auto Salvage. The truck features a roll bar and six-point roll cage for safety, a dashboard made of polished aluminum, Auto Meter gauges, and Smittybilt rear bumper. The body and name were painted by Rob Morris.

WILD HAIR!

"I BUILT IT IN MY DRIVEWAY!"

Wild Hair leaps
alongside Bigfoot during an indoor show
at Freedom Hall in Louisville, Kentucky.

Marvin Smith has been driving monster trucks over flattened junkers, through the mud and down the track with a pulling sled ever since the mid-1980s—and his professional experience behind the wheel doesn't end there. He used to pilot the Stomper II monster.

But monster trucks aren't the only vehicles he has driven in competition. Before beefing up his act to beastdom, Smith raced top eliminator drag cars and (you are reading this right) underwater Jeeps!

The Wild Hair monster, seen here mid-leap, is based on a Chevy Silverado Pickup. The custom modification was done mostly by Smith, who likes to stay close to home.

"I built it in my driveway," he says. That'll get the attention of the folks driving by!

The Wild Hair monster is powered by a Chevy 454 engine, which uses a big 871 supercharger and three Predator carburetors to produce 800 horsepower!

This power is routed to the tires via a Chevy Turbo 400 transmission (custom made by Transmissions-To-Go in Jefferson City, Missouri), Pro-Fab aluminum racing transfer case, and five-ton Rockwell axles with 20-ton planetary gears in the ends. The drivetrain turns the huge 66-inch-tall Goodyear Terra tires to give Smith the traction he needs to jump over cars and haul through the mud.

Smith has driven Wild Hair on the Camel Mud & Monster Series on ESPN television, and has toured with the United States Hot Rod Association's Camel Series.

PLAYIN' FOR KEEPS!

FAST OFF THE LINE!

While most monster trucks are built for power, here's a monster that's built for speed. Builder/owner Jesse Birgy has been building monster trucks for just about as long as there have been monster trucks. When Birgy became involved with the nationally televised TNT Monster Racing circuit, he designed his latest truck to excel in this high-powered racing competition.

The truck is based on a GMC S-15 pickup, but that's about as far as any similarity between Playin' For Keeps and any factory-made GMC goes. From there on, it's all custom made for speed and light weight.

Since the TNT races were often held indoors on short courses, the truck that can take off from the line the fastest (i.e. has the greatest power and the lightest weight) is often the winner.

With these requirements in mind, Birgy removed all of the inner body skin and panels. What you see is only the outer skin of the original vehicle. Unlike most racers, which use fiberglass bodies, Birgy felt that the real steel body of the GMC looks better and will last longer. The most major modification done to the original body was the addition of fender flares.

All Out For Power

While Birgy has tried to trim down on the body, with the motor he has gone all out for power. The engine is a 540-cubic-inch GMC big block, fed by two 1250 cfm Holley Dominator carbs on a 8-71 Littlefield Supercharger. This combo produces about—and this is a conservative estimate—1,100 horsepower.

Birgy's engine has stainless steel rocker arms, Competition Camshaft, titanium retainers. Childs/Albert aluminum rods, Victor gaskets, Pete Jackson gear drive, TRW pistons with ceramic rings and AFR titanium valves.

The 1,100 horsepower produced by this powerplant runs through a turbo hydramatic 474 transmission taken from a GMC motor home, then to a Timken T-136 airshift transfer case.

The front axle has a five-ton center with PS-250 Rockwell steering knuckles for increased strength. The rear has a straight five-ton axle and no longer steers. The truck runs 66-inch-tall Goodyear Terra tires on McCord steel wheels that are 38 inches wide.

These tires are kept under control by the new suspension system. The front axle has two stage springs with ladder bars, four Rough Country shocks per corner, and energy suspension bump stops.

The rear has leaf springs with ladder bars, three Rough Country shock absorbers per wheel, and energy suspension bump stops. The frame is made of heavy three- by six-inch rectangular tubing for rigidity. It's already taken a great deal of abuse, including a complete rollover, and is still perfectly straight.

Award-Winner For Safety

The interior of the truck and its MTRA safety features are outstanding. In fact, in its first year of competition, Playin' For Keeps won the MTRA Safety Award for the thoroughness and quality of its safety features. For example, it has Lexan plastic windows so there's no broken glass.

The cab has a Jaz racing seat locked in the center. It's also equipped with a RJS five-point racing harness, belts and pads. It has tachometer, oil-pressure and temperature gauges from Auto Meter, and a Moroso oil pressure warning light to warn Jesse when the oil pressure goes below 30 psi.

Birgy has the electrical system set up so that only two switches control everything. One switch is a universal ignition

While owner/driver Jesse Birgy has tried to trim down on Playin' For Keeps' body, with the motor he has gone all out for power. The engine is a 540-cubic-inch GMC big block, fed by two 1250 cfm Holley Dominator carbs on a 8-71 Littlefield Supercharger. This combo produces about 1,100 horsepower.

that starts, stops and controls the fan, electric water pump and ignition system. The other is a master kill switch that shuts down everything including the batteries. The transmission is controlled by a Fairbanks shifter. The truck's ignition is also set up to be shut off by the radio remote-control device used by TNT Motorsports, in case the truck gets out of the driver's control during a show and causes a safety hazard. While driving, Birgy is protected by a 12-point funny-car-style roll cage.

HANGIN' ON!

CORVETTE-POWERED!

Hangin' On is unusual because it was not originally purchased for conversion to a monster truck and because it's powered by a 1963 Chevy Corvette 327-cubic-inch engine.

This Chevy truck, Hangin' On, made its debut at the Iron-horse 4 x 4 March of Dimes Jammin' in July Mud Festival on July 15, 1990 in Crown Point, Indiana. That is, that was the first time both the truck, a 1974 Chevy Cheyenne Super 10, and its owner/driver Brian Welch, crushed cars and performed before crowds. But Welch has owned this truck since he was 16, and has been modifying the suspension and installing taller tires ever since. He's about reached the ultimate now, since the 66-inch-tall Goodyear Terra tires are the biggest you can buy!

The truck is unusual because it was not originally purchased for conversion to a monster truck. It's also unusual in that it's powered by a 1963 Chevy Corvette 327-cubic-inch engine. This engine puts out about 650 horsepower. It's been totally rebuilt to high-performance specifications, including a Predator carburetor, Wein aluminum intake, Cam Dynamics roller rockers, 202 Fuelie heads, Crane camshaft, Corello connecting rods, and 13:1 high-dome forged pistons. For extra horses, Brian has a Cheater series II nitrous-oxide system.

To fit those big tires on the truck, and to flatten cars with it, is another matter. To do this job, Welch has modified the suspension extensively and given the truck the lift it needs to carry the huge Goodyear Terra tires. This involved doing an eight-inch body lift, six-inch lift blocks, and installing five-ton military springs re-arched six inches. These are installed with five-ton military spring shackles and hangers.

To turn these huge tires, Welch has hooked up the Corvette engine's power to a Chevy 350 turbo transmission, an ATC 250 transfer case, and ten-ton Clark planetary ends on the five-ton military axles. This gives the Hangin' On monster maximum bullet-proof toughness.

It's all held together by the truck's original frame, extensively customized and reinforced to take the 11,500-pound weight of the truck. Now the Hangin' On Chevy has a 12-inch straight frame.

The beautiful paint job was done by Welch and his friend Andy. It has three-tone Imron, blue/black/gold with gold flecks over all. He's also installed a custom hydraulic tilt front end.

The interior also features complete Auto Meter gauges, two racing seats, RJS full harness, aluminum center console with rear steering controls, and an interior roll cage to meet MTRA safety requirements. The MTRA rules protect the crowd as well as Welch in the event of a rollover.

The vital statistics on the truck are that it's two feet six inches tall, twelve feet wide, has a 130-inch wheelbase (the original pickup was a shortbed) and it cost about $80,000 to build! Welch says it took him two years to put the entire truck together, working on weekends and in his spare time.

Look for Brian Welch at monster truck shows around the Midwest, where he'll be flattening cars and running mud bogs!

OVER EXCITED!

BEWARE THE LEAPING LADY!

Over Excited is the prized possession of husband-and-wife team, Doug and Shirley Harland of Woodstock, Illinois. Doug drives the truck during performances for now, but that's not going to be the case for long if Shirley has anything to say about it—and she does.

Shirley Harland is practicing car-jumping with Over Excited and plans to go public with her awesome stunts soon. Don't be too surprised. Monster truck stunts run in Shirley's family. She's the sister of Rob Fuchs, the driver of First Blood.

Over Excited is a monster truck with small, 48-inch Goodyear Terra tires, but don't let that fool you. Performance-wise, this yellow beauty is one mighty big truck!

It's based on a Chevrolet S-10 pickup body obtained with the help of Nelson's Auto Salvage—and it's Chevy-powered as well. Under the hood, the truck has a 402-cubic-inch Chevy big-block motor—with a Holley Strip Dominator intake manifold, Sid Erson Valvetrain, 12:1 compression pistons, steel crankshaft, Hooker headers and MSD ignition. It puts out about 450 horsepower, but this can be boosted instantly to 650 horsepower with a Compucar nitrous oxide injection system, supplied by Altered Egos of Woodstock.

Although the Harlands built most of the truck themselves, they did have some help. Mark Hartline of the Performance Off-Road Center in Huntley, Illinois installed the interior roll cage and supplied the Auto Meter gauges.

The tires were mounted, and are serviced, by Fischer Tire in Woodstock. The frame and other components were sandblasted by Magnuson Sandblasting in Woodstock.

The visor and cab extension are from Lund Industries. These contribute to the custom look of the truck. Finally, when all else was finished, the logo and signs were painted over the bright chrome yellow body color.

To support the 7,400-pound truck, Doug made a new frame from three- by five-inch steel tubing, which is made stronger and more rigid than frame rails. The suspension was designed by Len Manning of Spring-Align in Palatine, Illinois.

The drivetrain consists of a turbo 400 Chevy transmission built by Accurate Transmission of Arlington Heights, Illinois. This is connected to a one-and-a-half-ton Rockwell transfer case.

The front and rear axles are custom-narrowed, five-ton Rockwell military axles, which are steered hydraulically. Overall, the truck is ten feet tall, nine-and-a-half feet wide and has a 120-inch wheelbase.

This is Doug Harland behind the wheel—but his wife, Shirley Harland, is practicing car-jumping with Over Excited and plans to go public with her awesome stunts soon. Shirley is the sister of Rob Fuchs, the driver of the First Blood truck.

SUDDEN IMPACT!

15,500 POUNDS OF CRUSHING POWER!

The awesome Sudden Impact is owned by Greg Piontek of Cudahy, Wisconsin. It's built from a 1977 GMC long wheelbase pickup, and is powered by the huge 454-cubic-inch big-block Chevy motor. This is a supercharged engine. It has a 671 supercharger fed by two Predator racing carburetors with racing gas. This gives it an output of about 800 horsepower.

Other high-performance parts include Hooker headers and a Holley racing electric fuel pump. As you can see, Greg has no trouble launching its 15,500 pounds over cars.

The engine's power is fed via a turbo 400 GM transmission to a two-and-a-half-ton transfer case. Then it goes through the five-ton Rockwell axles to the Clark Planetaries. Mounted to the axles are the huge Goodyear Terra tires, each 66 inches tall, installed on McCord steel wheels. These are dampened by 20 shock absorbers made by Hecathorn (Heco).

Sudden Impact's paintwork was done by Bradco Co. of Cudahy, Wisconsin. While most of the monster trucks today are stripping

Sudden Impact is built from a 1977 GMC long-wheelbase pickup, and is powered by the huge 454-cubic-inch big-block Chevy motor.

Sudden Impact has a
671 supercharger fed by two Predator racing
carburetors with racing gas. This gives it an output of about 800 horsepower.

themselves of chrome accessories to save weight, Sudden Impact is still a customized truck. It has Bushwacker fender flares, a hydraulic tilting front end, a Westin double-tube chrome rear bumper, and a Warn chrome front-winch bumper.

The interior was done by America's Choice, and includes seats and tonneau cover by Dave Kasper. It also has Auto meter gauges inside, a Hobrecht chrome in-cab roll cage, and a racing seat. Piontek would like to thank sponsors Creative

Customs Off-Road Center and Five Corners GMC for their assistance.

You may have seen Sudden Impact perform all over the Midwest for Rev and the American Tough Truck Association. It can also been seen at the Great Lakes Dragaway in Union Grove, Wisconsin where Broadway Bob puts on a great show during his "Fun Truckin' Weekends."

BLACKHAWK!

WISCONSIN GMC MONSTER!

Blackhawk was built and is owned by Greg Piontek of Cudahy, Wisconsin, a suburb of Milwaukee. Greg is in the off-road customizing business and runs an off-road shop called ''Creative Customs Off-Road Center.'' He's seen the big monsters racing at the local Great Lakes Dragaway and decided to show off some of his own truck-customizing expertise. The result is the beautiful and awesome Blackhawk.

The truck took ten months to build and was constructed by Piontek and his friends Wally and Brian. For the truck's body, they decided to showcase the classic 1977 GMC long wheelbase pickup. Many four-wheel drive pickup fans can remember the styling of the 1970s Chevy and Ford trucks.

But the original 1977 GMC pickup and Blackhawk are two entirely different animals. Piontek started to convert the pickup to a monster by re-building the frame. This involved reinforc-

ing it with steel plate and channel to make it stronger and provide mounting points for the springs and shocks.

Next came the suspension. Blackhawk has military springs, with additional eight inches of lift given by custom-made lift blocks. There are five shock absorbers over each wheel, 20 in all. Blackhawk uses the yellow Hecathorn ''Heco'' shocks.

Next came the powerplant and drivetrain. Blackhawk is powered by the huge 454-cubic-inch block Chevy engine, which uses two Predator racing carburetors that provide racing gas to a 671 supercharger. The fuel is pumped with a Holley racing fuel pump. Chrome Hooker headers give the monstrous engine the breathing power it needs. This engine produces about 800 honest horsepower, and judging from the way Piontek can leap the 15,500-pound behemoth onto cars, 800 horsepower is probably a conservative number.

These horses are routed through a custom-made GM turbo 400 transmission, to a two-and-a-half-ton military transfer case. Then, custom-made, heavy-duty drive shafts send it to the five-ton Rockwell military axles. The u-joints enter the differential from the top. These are the ''toploader'' differentials seen on military trucks. Clark planetary gears, taken from heavy equipment, provide the final turning power to the hubs. They are virtually break-proof.

Blackhawk uses the huge 66-inch-tall Goodyear Terra tires, mounted on steel wheels custom made by McCord Tire of Monticello, Indiana.

The Beauty in the Beast!

So much for the brawn. Now for the beauty: Blackhawk has been customized with the kind of accessories you'd find on a small four-wheel drive pickup. These include cut-out fender

flares, a Custom tilting front end, a Westin double-tube roll bar, nine KC Daylighter lights up on top, a twelve-inch Westin chrome rear bumper, and a Warn chrome front winch bumper.

The interior has been done by America's Choice of West Allis, Wisconsin, and the seats and tonneau cover are by Dave Kasper. The dashboard features Auto Meter gauges, and a Hobrecht chrome in-cab cage kit for safety.

All in all, Blackhawk measures a monstrous 11 feet tall, 11 feet six inches wide, and 18 feet long. It cost about $40,000 to build (in parts alone.) Piontek would like to thank Five Corners GMC and Creative Customs Off-Road Center for their assistance. He and Blackhawk perform all over the Midwest.

For the truck's body, Greg Piontek decided to showcase the classic 1977 GMC long-wheelbase pickup. Blackhawk cost about $40,000 to build—in parts alone!

GOLIATH!

LIKE A SNORTING BULL!

Goliath is one monster truck that truly lives up to its name! Alan Tura—from Warren, Ohio—got the itch to build a monster when he saw Bigfoot at the Pontiac Silverdome. At the time, he was on the pit crew for the Magnum Force pulling truck and said, "I gotta get me one!"

At the time, there were only a few giant trucks out. Tura wanted to get in on the monster-truck market on the ground floor. The second he finished building Goliath, he started to get bookings, so the Tura/Goliath team went right to work—averaging more than 40 weeks on the road a year.

Tura says he always tries to stay one step ahead with fresh ideas to keep his truck at the head of the four-wheel drive and pulling circuit.

During a show, Tura enjoys stunning the crowd by climbing onto the roof of his truck and waving to the crowd while the truck is going down the track.

With pipes on the front belching smoke out, Goliath looks like a snorting bull!

Goliath is Big Screen Friendly!

With 600 Vista Versa marker lites, two B.D.S. Supercharge 460 Ford engines and 14 remote-control KC Daylighters, we can see what Tura means.

Take note, Hollywood! Tura says he has been collecting notes during his past five years of travel, and he is looking for a screenwriter and producer to turn his story into, as they say, a major motion picture.

What makes Goliath tick? That's simple. First, there's an 18,000-pound suspension, with Clark Planetary axles. Reider Racing Enterprises gear seats in the axles. Rugged Trail suspension shocks control the bounce, and there's a Ramsey winch—just in case the going gets too tough!

The engines were prepared by Rich Shargo of Rick's Automotive Machine in Masury, Ohio. Rick used high-performance parts such as Arias pistons, Sealed Power rings and bearings, Crane cams, Hedman headers to control the exhaust, Ronco magnetos that can put out a spark that will knock your socks off, a Cloyes timing chain for improved cam-to-crank time, Fel-Pro gaskets to seal it tight, Predator carbs to fuel the B.D.S. Blowers and presto—you get 1,000 horsepower of engine with a cost of $15,000 per engine. With Reflexions bumpers, Hobrecht roller bars, Dee Zee running boards, a Dupont Mariner Imron Blue painted by Maaco Paint Works, and a good Turtle Wax polish applied, Goliath really rolls! The tires are 66- by 43- by 25-inch Firestone Floatations 23—with a good application of Armor All protectant to keep them looking smooth and clean.

Tura is thankful to A.T.I. Transmissions, Mac Tools, Ed's Sandblasting, Cartell Octane Booster, Hadley Air Horns, Kendall Oil, and all of his other sponsors for their support.

What makes Goliath tick? That's simple. First, there's an 18,000-pound suspension, with Clark Planetary axles. Reider Racing Enterprises gear seats in the axles. Rugged Trail suspension shocks control the bounce, and there's a Ramsey winch—just in case the going gets too tough!

WHISKEY BUSINESS!

TURNING BOOZE INTO CHEERS!

This Chevy Monster, Whiskey Business, was built by Jon Breen of Jefferson City, Missouri who has been in the monster-truck racing field for years. Breen has always built Chevy monsters. His first racing style monster was Mad Dog, which some of you older monster-truck fans might remember.

Although this monster racer was built by Breen, it's driven by Ken Deppe of Morrison, Missouri. Deppe is hardly new to the racing business either. He built a racing Bronco with Breen back in 1980.

The Power's In The Rear!

The Whiskey Business monster racer is built on a Chevy C10 pickup body. It has a custom-built, heavy-duty suspension using leaf springs and 20 Hecathorn shock absorbers, five on each wheel. The huge Goodyear 66-inch-tall tires are mounted on steel wheels. The axles are the big five-ton Rockwell military type with Case 1200 differentials.

To power Whiskey Business, Breen installed a high-performance 468-cubic-inch Chevy engine. It is fueled by alcohol, injected by an Enderle injection system and a tunnel ram. It develops about 750 horsepower and has 12.5:1 pistons, a Lunatic camshaft and crankshaft, an Enderle fuel pump, and an MSD ignition system.

The unusual feature of the engine is that it's mounted on the rear of Whiskey Business. Breen did this so that "it flies and lands better." The rear-engine keeps the weight in the rear, where it will help balance the truck better while it bounces into cars.

The beautiful graphics and lettering were done by Smith Sign of Sedalia, Missouri. The interior is basically stock, with the addition of some high-performance racing gauges.

The seats are Cerullo Racing seats, and it is fully MTRA safety equipped. This includes the remote control kill switch, roll bar, interior roll cage, fire extinguisher, etc. Whiskey Business has been seen on TV running with the Camel Mud & Monster Series for the United States Hot Rod Association.

The unusual feature of the engine is that it's mounted on the rear of Whiskey Business. Breen did this so that "it flies and lands better." The rear engine keeps the weight in the rear, where it will help balance the truck better while it bounces into cars.

APOCALYPSE NOW!

CHOPPER MONSTER!

This unique, awesome monster was built with a real helicopter body. It was constructed by Damian Dominsky of Cudahy, Wisconsin.

Dominsky says he had wanted to build a monster truck with a helicopter body for some time, but had trouble locating a genuine helicopter body.

Finally, he found one in Missouri. The owner had several, and probably wouldn't have parted with it had he known what Dominsky *really* intended to do with it. But, he finally gave in and sold it to Dominsky, who trucked the body home to Cudahy for conversion into a monster truck.

The helicopter body is from a 1970 Bell 206 Jet Ranger. It was powered by jet turbine engines. But Dominsky bought only what you see here. The first thing Dominsky did was set the helicopter body on a custom frame made of three- by six-inch rectangular tubing. The frame length gave him a wheelbase of 132 inches.

To this frame he has installed a Ford 460-cubic-inch engine. It uses Predator carburetors, Offenhauser Port-O-Sonic

Owner/builder Damian Dominsky set the helicopter body on a custom frame made of three- by six-inch rectangular tubing. As you can see here, the body raises up hydraulically, and can be driven with the body raised up!

Apocalypse Now's helicopter body is from a 1970 Bell 206 Jet Ranger.

manifold, Mallory Unilite distributor and Cyclone heads. All of the engine mounts, frame brackets, wiring, fuel line, dashboard wiring, gauges, etc., had to be custom fitted by Dominsky. The dash has water temperature, ammeter, and oil-pressure gauges.

Ready For Takeoff!

The driver has RJS lap-and-shoulder harnesses for safety. The inside of the Chopper Monster is huge. It has a rear bench seat and can seat five. It's really a weird feeling sitting in this monster, since the body is all-helicopter. The truck is so high off the ground that you feel you're about to take off!

The Chopper Monster is set in motion by a Ford C6 transmission with street fight converter, operated with a B & M shifter kit. The power then runs to a two-and-a-half-ton transfer case. It has pettibone axles and 66-inch-tall Firestone tires.

These huge, heavy tires are dampened by leaf springs in the front with 12 leaves, and five-leaf springs in the rear. Four Rugged Trail shock absorbers (the Monster type) are over each wheel.

The Chopper Monster is ten feet tall, weighs 11,000 pounds and is 17 feet long to the end of the boom. It's painted the light olive drab color inside, while the outside is official NATO Camouflage! The body raises up hydraulically, and can be driven while raised up! Dominsky plans to install an awesome sound system (on which he'll play Wagner's "Ride of the Valkyries," from the attack scene in the movie *Apocalypse Now*.) He might also hook up some rockets and exploding bombs to attack the cars! In the meantime, Dominsky is using the beast to crush cars, the same as other monsters.

To the frame, Damian Dominsky has installed a Ford 460-cubic-inch engine.

Chopper Monster's huge interior seats five!

BARBARIAN!

WHAT? A CHEVY-POWERED FORD?

Ask the fans at a monster truck show what they like better, Fords or Chevys, and you're most likely to come up with a 50-50 response. Maybe it depends on where in the country you live—some parts of the country are decidedly Ford Country, and vice-versa.

So, to please everybody, Jim Miller built his original, 1979 Ford pickup monster with a Chevy engine! This way, Jim figured, he got the best of both worlds: the Ford body styling he liked and the Chevy power he wanted.

Of course, there are plenty of people who can get lots of horsepower out of Ford engines. Consider the Bigfoot people, for example. They run awesome, supercharged Ford engines.

But Miller was able to get his engine built by Kirns Racing Motors of St. Louis, Missouri. It's a racing motor shop not too far from Miller's southern Illinois hometown of Nokomis.

Older Bodies Better

The truck is built on a 1979 Ford pickup body. Miller prefers the older pickup body because of its stronger cab and thicker sheet metal. The new pickups have such thin sheet metal that they quickly develop stress wrinkles when the monsters launch over cars—and when they land.

The truck is painted in orange enamel, with a special Barbarian logo on the doors. It has full MTRA safety equipment, including a Smittybilt roll bar and cage.

Blast Off!

Back in the old days, Barbarian ran a 454 big-block Chevy motor that had been supercharged. The powerplant was fuel-injected with alcohol, to produce about 1,000 horsepower. When this motor was first put in, Miller couldn't believe

The 490-cubic-inch Chevy engine cranks out the 1,200 horsepower necessary to send Barbarian into orbit.

When this new motor was first put in, Miller couldn't believe the extra power he had. He said, "All I have to do is touch that gas pedal about an eighth of an inch and the truck launches into the air!" You can see from the photos what he was talking about.

the extra power he had. He said, "All I have to do is touch that gas pedal about an eighth of an inch and the truck launches into the air!" You can see from the photos what he was talking about.

Now Miller has further upped the ante.

Miller's new powerplant is a 490-cubic-inch Chevy engine, supercharged and fuel injected. It produces a whopping 1,200 horsepower! Miller says he now has more power than ever— and the truck zooms into the air, ready to clear any obstacle! The new engine was built by Fred Shafer, owner of the Bear Foot trucks.

To save a little weight, Miller now uses an aluminum military transfer case, which runs 1:1 gearing into the two driveshafts. The driveshaft, in turn, runs into Rockwell five-ton axles with Clark 20-ton planetary gear on the ends. The planetaries make the axles virtually break-proof. Mounted to the axles are Goodyear 66-inch-tall tires, on McCord steel wheels.

Lean and Clean!

The truck has now slimmed down to 13,000 pounds, which is light for the older Rockwell-axled trucks, but still heavy compared to the trucks that run monster-truck obstacle courses.

However, on straight runs, Miller can hold his own, due to his extra horsepower. The Barbarian's orange body was painted by Jerry Loskot, and the truck has a triple roll bar and heavy-steel bumpers on the front and rear.

The interior is customized, with brown velour fabric on the seats and door panels, and Sun gauges. These help Miller keep an eye on the engine's performance during races. Miller figures that the truck cost him $80,000 to build!

Overall, Jim Miller has been in the monster-truck business longer than most drivers—almost ten years. He and Barbarian have performed with the United States Hot Rod Association all over the country!

ALL CANADIAN!

MONSTER FROM NORTH OF THE BORDER!

All of the monster trucks that you have seen in this book were made in the U.S.A. As most of you know, Bigfoot was the first Ford monster truck, and it's from the St. Louis area. Fred Shafer's Bear Foot is the original Chevy monster truck.

But now our Canadian friends to the north are getting into monsters. For years, they've been importing monster trucks for truck shows, but now they've got two homegrown beasts. A resident of Timmins, Ontario by the name of Frenchy Cloutier has built *both* a monster with rubber tires and a tank monster. Here we will feature the older of the two, the rubber-tire vehicle.

Cloutier has a long history of building racing machines. In the past 24 years he has raced everything from snowmobiles in the winter to diesel trucks and speedboats that exceed 200 mph on the water.

He spent one-and-a-half years perfecting All Canadian, which is based on a 1981 Dodge Club Cab.

Stable While Crushing!

To support and stabilize the anticipated weight of the truck while crushing cars, Frenchy and his friends built a ten-inch-tall custom frame.

The truck is powered by a 600 horsepower Detroit Diesel engine. The transmission is a Fuller five-speed, and the transfer case is a double-reduction Rockwell.

The driveshafts are heavy-wall driveshafts taken from a Mack truck. These feed into Rockwell five-ton top mount military differentials.

Planetary gears are used on the ends of the axles. Both front and rear axles steer hydraulically, and eight Monroe stabilizer shocks help stabilize the steering system while the All Canadian is crushing cars.

Durability, Strength & Safety!

The suspension is custom-made using truck springs. These are softened by 20 heavy-duty Monroe shock absorbers. The big Firestone 66- by 43- by 25-inch tires are used, and these are mounted on custom-made heavy-duty steel rims.

All of these parts—the engine, drivetrain and axles—were carefully chosen and fitted to the truck to provide the best in durability, strength and safety.

On the outside, many modifications and accessories have been made to make the All Canadian look like a custom show truck. It has a hydraulic lift box, tinted sun roof, visor, molly triple chrome roll bars, 16 chrome spotlights mounted on the roll bar, and eight, three-inch chrome exhaust heads which angle forward out of the massive engine. The pickup box is topped with a chrome rail and custom tonneau cover.

The interior is heavily customized, with a racing steering wheel, ten gauges on the dashboard, two velour captain's chairs, and custom diamond-pleated fabric on the floors, doors and ceiling. Overall, All Canadian weighs 18,000 pounds, stands 12 feet six inches tall, 12 feet six inches wide, and is 20 feet long! It's truly a vehicle of *monstrous* proportions.

Frenchy Cloutier has a long history of building racing machines. In the past 24 years he has raced everything from snowmobiles in the winter to diesel trucks and speedboats that exceed 200 mph on the water. So the monster truck idea came naturally to him.

HEAVY METAL THUNDER!

ILLINOIS BIG-BLOCK CHEVY!

Heavy Metal Thunder was built by Dennis Norton Sr. and Dennis Norton Jr. of McHenry, Illinois. It's based on a 1980 GMC pickup body—but has been completely rebuilt to do monster truck car crushing, jumps, and sled pulling.

Under the hood, there is a Chevy big block 454-cubic-inch motor, fed by two high-performance Predator racing carburetors on a Weiand tunnel ram.

The engine was bored .30 over. It has 11:1 TRW pistons,

heads ported and matched to the intake manifold, Manley valves, a steel crankshaft, Pete Jackson gear drive, and Crane hydraulic camshaft.

It produces about 500 horsepower. The drivetrain is made up of a GM turbo 400 transmission with manual valve body. The differentials are 10.26:1. These turn the big 48- by 25- by 20-inch Super Terra tires mounted on steel rims.

To hold the engine and drivetrain together, the Nortons

Heavy Metal Thunder is based on a 1980 GMC pickup body—but has been completely rebuilt to do monster truck car crushing, jumps, and sled pulling. The engine is a Chevy big block 454-cubic-inch motor, fed by two high-performance Predator racing carburetors on a Weiand tunnel ram.

have rebuilt the frame and beefed it up. The stock frame was plated with 3/16-inch steel plate reinforced with steel tubing. There are extra cross members at stress points, while the body has been kept stock. The suspension features Boyce springs and hangers, and has four Rancho shock absorbers per wheel.

The interior has been modified for racing, with a full roll cage for safety, Sun Tachometer, factory electric gauges, single Jaz fiberglass bucket seat, B&M Pro Stick Shifter, fire extinguisher and five-point Pyrotech harness. The interior, however, still has the original factory dashboard and door panels.

The Nortons have performed with Heavy Metal Thunder in the northern Illinois/Wisconsin area, and have worked for Broadway Bob at Great Lakes Dragaway in Union Grove, Wisconsin, as well as Rev and American Motorsports Unlimited.

TAURUS!

SNORTIN' AND CHARGIN'!

This monster race truck has been terrorizing fans and monster owners alike—Jack Willman's Taurus! The fans are awed by the truck's tremendous speed and handling ability, while the other monster truck owners are complaining that it can't be beat. Many, in fact, are refusing to perform against it! Since Taurus first appeared, it has won more than 90% of its races. Its only losses were caused by minor mechanical problems.

The Taurus truck was engineered by Dave Cook, an engineer who has worked for Allis Chalmers. It's based on a 1989 truck body, but it's made of fiberglass to save weight. Using fiberglass, made by Creative Glass of Tennessee, saves several hundred pounds of weight in the truck body alone. Other parts of the interior, such as the dashboard, are made of weight-saving aluminum.

The engine is a Chevy 468 big-block engine, with a 671 Hilborn injection system. The ignition system is by MSD, and it uses an Ultradyne camshaft. The fuel-in

jected powerplant is fueled by alcohol. Several years ago, Taurus was one of the first trucks to run on alcohol. The engine produces about 1,000 honest horsepower. The power is fed through a turbo 400 transmission and ProFab aluminum transfer case to both axles.

But the engine alone isn't what makes the truck run so well. In addition to the truck's light weight (only 7900 lbs.), it also has a unique set of axles and suspension system. The axles cost $15,000 apiece new, but their exact brand name is kept a secret. They have 5.30:1 gear ratios in the differentials, and planetary gears in the ends. Both axles are steering axles.

The suspension system is the newest, most radical aspect of Taurus. It's a completely new design, using a coil-over shock-absorber system, and a four-link suspension. It has an incredible 18 inches of travel. This enables the truck to fly over cars without bouncing excessively, giving greater control to the driver. Taurus can make turns and maneuver through obstacle courses faster than any other monster truck.

The beautifully painted body has been painted in the traditional Taurus color of berry red Imron with Aztec gold yellow and a pearl white stripe, by Butch Ragsdale. The interior is stripped-down for racing, and includes a Super Seat.

MTRA safety equipment, and Auto Meter gauges. With Taurus, Jack Willman has a truck that's definitely the one to beat. In fact, other truck builders are making their new trucks lighter and faster to compete with Taurus.

Bear Foot unsuccessfully attempts to break Taurus' phenominal winning streak.

BLACK STALLION!

UNCHAIN THE NIGHT!

The Black Stallion was built by owner/operator Michael Vaters of Hagerstown, Maryland. This ebony beauty sports a Ford F250 body—which was supplied by Ed Blask Ford of Yorkville, New York.

Under its exterior, the Stallion sports a 460 engine, bored out .30 over, with a tunnel ram, two Predator carburetors, C-6 automatic transmission and a two-and-a-half-ton military transfer case.

Throw in five-ton military axles with 14-inch Clark planetary hubs, 16 rugged trail shocks and Goodyear 66-inch-tall tires, and you've got the makings of one awesome vehicle.

The Black Stallion is
clearly the Cadillac of monster trucks.

Black Stallion sports a Ford F250 body. An Alpine stereo with two BOSE amps and ten speakers keeps the tunes cranking while the Black Stallion does its thing. There's a three-inch color TV installed in the dash!

The Black Stallion is clearly the Cadillac of monster trucks. All removable parts are chromed or glossy black, the cab interior is resplendent with grey velour, and an Alpine stereo with two BOSE amps and ten speakers keeps the tunes cranking while the Black Stallion does its thing.

And for those times when the Black Stallion rolls over the competition too quickly, don't worry—there's a three-inch color TV installed in the dash, so Vaters can watch the whole thing on instant replay!

The Black Stallion has gained a reputation as a vehicle to watch. And you may just get the opportunity. The pitch-colored beast has been performing to packed houses throughout the United States, Canada and the Bahamas. Keep your eyes peeled—the Black Stallion could be coming for you!

Under its exterior, the Stallion sports a 460 engine, bored out .30 over, with a tunnel ram, two predator carburetors, a C-6 automatic transmission and a two-and-a-half-ton military transfer case.

The Black Stallion has gained a reputation as a vehicle to watch.

Owner/operator Michael Vaters of Hagerstown, Maryland waves to the crowd. Black Stallion has performed to packed houses throughout the United States, Canada and the Bahamas.

BLACK STALION

BURNIN' DESIRE!

IT'S GOT A THING FOR FIRE!

Since it was first built, Burnin' Desire has had a thing for fire! The first version of the truck was called Red Devil. It performed at the Great Lakes Dragaway in Union Grove, Wisconsin—until one day when it caught on fire and burned!

Then the truck was rebuilt by Bill Lynch, on a Chevy Blazer body with a big-block Chevy 454-cubic-inch engine. Lynch named it Burnin' Desire. As you can see in the photos, this truck also goes for smoke and flame!

After the truck burned two years ago, Lynch decided to completely rebuild it. With the help of the Rescue 1 4x4 club, he was able to tow the truck to and from the various

Over several years and a couple of incarnations, this truck has always had a thing for smoke and flame.

At this performance, the Amazing Spiderman made his entrance atop Burnin' Desire.

shops that helped him with the rebuilding job. These included Image Auto Body, who helped in the rebuilding work, Endeavor Recycling, who helped sponsor the rebuilding, and All-Car Automotive, who helped by supplying parts and accessories.

With the help of these sponsors, Lynch was able to redo the 1987 Chevy Blazer to the condition it's in today.

810 hp ... Without the Nitrous!

The engine is a Chevy 454 with roller rockers, a new camshaft, 12.5:1 aluminum pistons, 1053 steel crankshaft, hardened push rods, Predator carburetors, Edelbrock Torker II manifold, Nitrous oxide, Hooker Competition headers, and Edelbrock chrome valve covers. This engine produces about 810 horsepower, without the nitrous!

The engine was built by B&S Engines of Kingston, Wisconsin by Nick and Bill, with help from Brian Schwandt.

The transmission is a turbo 400 with reverse manual valve body, installed by Lynch. It's linked to a military two-and-a-half-ton transfer case, feeding two military two-and-a-half-ton axles. On these two axles are mounted big 54-inch-tall Goodyear Tires.

The body painting was done by Lynch at Image Auto Body in Kingston, Wisconsin. The suspension has 16 Rancho shock absorbers, mounted on a suspension consisting of a stock military truck suspension, beefed up by Lynch.

The interior of the truck used to be a stock Blazer interior, but now it has new silver-cloth upholstery and an interior roll cage. It has the MTRA safety equipment, designed to keep the driver, vehicle, and fans safe at all times.

Lynch did a lot of the work himself, but is grateful to the above mentioned sponsors for their invaluable assistance.

LIQUIDATOR!

JERSEY GIANT!

Monster-truck fans who live in the Eastern part of the country should be familiar with the Liquidator monster Ford. It's been running on the monster-truck circuit for years. It was first built by Bob Fisher in 1988.

Since that time, Fisher—who is the president of Garden State Monster Trucks Inc.—has constantly improved the truck, making little changes to the body, accessories, and engine. The Liquidator truck you see here is built out of a Ford

Photographer Mike Bargo offers a spectacular view of Liquidator doing its thing!

Liquidator is built out of a Ford Super Duty truck body. Liquidator has a 460-cubic-inch Ford powerplant, fed by two Predator high-performance carburetors and a tunnel ram.

Super Duty truck body. It has a 460-cubic-inch Ford power-plant, fed by two Predator high-performance carburetors and a tunnel ram.

It also has a host of high-performance parts, including a Weiland manifold, TRW pistons, heavy-duty truck connecting rods, Crane camshaft, Fram oil filter, and a Mallory Unilite distributor with MSD box, provided by one of the Liquidator's sponsors, Auto Parts Connection of Mt. Holly, New Jersey.

The engine breathes with the help of headers built by Mike Wales at Hannums Garage in Vineland, New Jersey. This engine puts out about 400 honest horsepower.

To build the Ford into a monster truck, Fisher had to first build a monster-size frame. He did this by fabricating a custom frame out of a three- by five-inch rectangular steel tubing. Then he installed the engine and drivetrain, which consists of a Ford C-6 truck transmission, a two-and-a-half-ton Rockwell

airshift military transfer case, and five-ton military Rockwell axles with Clark planetary gears in the ends.

The suspension is made up of custom-arched leaf springs specially designed for the Liquidator, and 18 Trail Master shock absorbers. The tires are the 66-inch-tall Goodyear Terras, mounted on steel wheels.

The bright paint color of the Liquidator truck is Peterbilt yellow, the same paint used to build Peterbuilt tractors. The truck also has a chrome roll bar with six KC Hilighter lights and a chrome Warn winch bumper up front.

The interior features two Cerullo monster truck seats, and a dashboard full of Auro Meter gauges, provided by Auto Parts Connection.

One unusual feature of the truck is that it has a two-way communication system between the driver and the crew, sponsored by Birch's Communications of May's Landing, New Jersey.

VIRGINIA BEACH BEAST!

THE ORIGINAL MONSTER TANK!

Look out, obstacles of the world! Here comes the original monster tank—Virginia Beach Beast! This is a tracked vehicle that crushes cars just like a monster truck.

Although dozens of these monster tanks have sprouted up all over the country, the very first one was built by Willie Townes of Norfolk, Virginia.

This beast is a Chevy-powered vehicle. The engine is a big-block Chevy 454, supercharged by a 671 blower and fed by two Predator racing carburetors, to produce about 1,000 horsepower!

These 1,000 horses are routed through a high-performance, specially modified turbo 400 automatic transmission, then fed into the gearbox of the track set. This gearbox is located in front of the tank tracks, and drives the vehicle forward.

The Virginia
Beach Beast has been performing
since January of 1986, and is still going strong,
doing stunts all around the country.

The track set is from a 1940s M4 personnel carrier,
used during World War II.

From WWII to an Arena Near You!

The track set is from a 1940s M4 personnel carrier used during World War II. These personnel carriers were so durable that they were brought back after the war and are still in excellent condition.

All you have to do is hook a driveshaft up to the gearbox and you're ready to go! Of course, fabricating a body, transmission mount, and other important parts take a lot of ingenuity and work, and credit must go to Townes to be the first person to be able to put this all together.

The Virginia Beach Beast has been performing since January of 1986, and is still going strong, doing stunts all around the country. It weighs about 23,000 pounds, and is ten feet tall.

It's so heavy that when it pounces on cars, it doesn't just dent them—it flattens them into sheet metal!

It has a very low center of gravity, and turns on a dime. If you want to turn left, you pull the left brake handle. This slows down the left side track, while the right side keeps on going. The result is that the tank turns to the left. The same procedure (in reverse, of course) is followed to turn the tank to the right.

The Virginia Beach Beast has been performing since January of 1986, and is still going strong, doing stunts all around the country.

Townes would like to thank his sponsors, Perfect Circle, Victor Gaskets, Permatex, Loctite, Duro, Centerline Engineering, and NOS for their support. You can see Townes performing all over the United States with his Virginia Beach Beast, the original and still the most awesome monster tank!

It weighs about 23,000 pounds, and is ten feet tall.

Virginia Beach Beast, the original monster tank,
is so heavy that when it pounces on cars, it doesn't just
dent them—it flattens them like pizzas!
It does a number on this bus, too!

SAMSON I

ROLLOVER TIME!

Don Maples, of Huntsville, Alabama, bills Samson I as "the World's Largest 4X4X4," and he may just be right—it's certainly the world's meanest! Originally a 1985 Chevrolet Silverado, the "revised" Samson I now stands 14 feet high and takes up twelve and a half feet of road width-wise.

At over 19,000 lbs.,
there are few vehicles that can match the mauling power
of Samson I.

Like the legendary Samson of
old, this giant smashes
through mud, over cars, and
generally destroys anything
that gets in its way. Take a tip
from an insider—if you see
Samson I coming, get out
of the way!

Bounty Hunter!

OUTLAWS BEWARE! HERE IT COMES . . .

The Bounty Hunter is a Chevy monster truck owned by Brian and Leann Bellini of Dixon, Illinois. It's based on a 1979 Chevy shortbed one-half-ton pickup truck, but the resemblance to the stock Chevy pickup ends there. It's been heavily rebuilt in the frame and drivetrain to fit the big axles, tires, and springs needed to run the monster-truck circuit.

The engine is a high-performance Chevy 350, aspirated by a high-performance Predator carburetor. Right now, the engine puts out 300 horsepower, but Brian has plans to replace it soon with a 427-cubic-inch powerplant. This will double the horsepower of the Bounty Hunter.

The drivetrain is a turbo 350 transmission, hooked to a New Process 203 transfer case and a two-and-a-half-ton Reo transfer case. The two-and-a-half-ton Rockwell axles are used, with gear ratios at 6.72:1. Big 25- by 30-inch wheels are used to mount the huge Firestone 66- by 43- by 25-inch tires. These huge tires are controlled by Rugged Trail shocks.

It also has a full roll cage, custom roll bar, hydraulically powered tilt front end, chrome bumpers, and one million candle power in the lights. The truck is eleven feet tall, eleven feet wide, and weighs 13,000 pounds.

The Bounty Hunter has performed for the United States Hot Rod Association at shows in the Midwest.

The Bounty Hunter is beautifully painted in a Porsche Red, with the Bounty Hunter name in yellow and orange neon-style lettering, and a pink neon stripe down each side.

The stock Chevy pickup has been heavily rebuilt in the frame and drivetrain to fit the big axles, tires, and springs needed to run the monster-truck circuit.

GODZILLA!

KING OF MONSTERS!

"**H**istory shows again and again how nature points out the folly of man—GODZILLA!"

So sang Blue Oyster Cult and those words are still true today. Especially in the case of one green-skinned monster from Rhode Island: Godzilla.

Originally a Ford F250 pickup, this baby has come a long way since then. A perennial favorite at car-crushing exhibitions, this awesome machine is the product of the sweat and determination of Alvin Thurber Jr. and his son Alvin III.

A perennial favorite at car-crushing exhibitions, this awesome machine is the product of the sweat and determination of Alvin Thurber Jr., and his son Alvin III. Godzilla weighs in at an unbelievable ten tons!

After mangling a few cars, Godzilla flexes its muscle a bit, raises its hood and displays some impressive artwork. This monster weighs in at an unbelievable ten tons, from its five-foot-tall tires to its reinforced five-ton military chassis. Owned and operated by the Thurbers' company, A & A Enterprises, of Pawtucket, Rhode Island, the King of Monsters keeps its masters' hands full living up to its busy promotion schedule.

So watch out Tokyo, and the rest of the world—Godzilla is coming!

ROCKY MOUNTAIN THUNDER

COLORADO PEAK PEFORMANCE!

Rocky Mountain Thunder is a Ford monster owned by Nick and Michele Jackson of Grand Junction, Colorado. The truck is based on a Ford F-150 pickup body, but was completely rebuilt to monster-size by Dave W. and Nick.

Rocky Mountain Thunder has a 454-cubic-inch powerplant, fed by two Predator racing carburetors and a tunnel ram. Its high-performance internal engine parts (12.9:1 TRW pistons, a Competition camshaft, and a Mallory Super Mag II to provide the spark) enable it to produce 600 horsepower.

These horses are fed through a Neil Chane turbo 400 au-

Rocky Mountain Thunder's body has a lot of custom mural paintwork. The body was painted a beautiful red garnet poly color, then the mountain mural was added by Hot Flash Customs of Grand Junction.

Its high-performance internal engine parts (12.9:1 TRW pistons, a Competition camshaft, and a Mallory Super Mag II to provide the spark) enable it to produce 600 horsepower. There are 18 shock absorbers used on the monster—five over each front wheel, to take the shock of car crushing, and four over each rear wheel.

tomatic transmission, rebuilt to high-performance specifications, then a two-and-a-half-ton airshift military transfer case to route the power to the two driveshafts.

The driveshafts run to the two, big, five-ton Rockwell axles, which have ten-ton planetary gears in the ends. Finally, the axles turn the huge Goodyear Terra tires, which are five and a half feet tall, mounted on steel wheels.

The wheels are mounted under Rocky Mountain Thunder by a leaf spring suspension. There are 18 shock absorbers used on the monster—five over each front wheel to take the shock of car crushing, and four over each rear wheel.

All of this driving gear and suspension hardware is sup-

ported by the big frame of the truck, which was custom made by Nick out of 3- by 8-inch rectangular tubing.

The truck has a lot of customized accessories and equipment, making it one of the most customized monsters around. This includes a lot of custom chrome-plated parts, done by Swedes Custom Chrome of Grand Junction, Colorado.

Nick says the chrome-plating custom work is worth $7,000, and everything that could be chromed under the truck was chromed. Such items as the driveline, shock absorbers, driveline loops, and planetary hubs are all chrome plated, giving the truck a sleek custom-show look. Rocky Mountain Thunder also has a custom double-chrome roll bar and lights.

UNNAMED & UNTAMED!

1942 DODGE POWER WAGON MONSTER!

While all newer monster trucks have fiberglass bodies, tubular frames and four-point suspensions, Unnamed & Untamed is a refreshing throwback to the solidly built trucks of the 1940s.

Unnamed & Untamed, a unique monster truck from Portland, Oregon, is built from a 1942 Dodge Power Wagon body—although it's powered by a Chevy engine!

When the Unnamed & Untamed truck was first built, it was one of the lightest monster trucks around at 9,700 lbs., even though it had the old steel sheet metal body.

It also has one of the longest (if not *the* longest) wheelbases of any monster truck: 150 inches. This extra-long wheelbase —achieved by mounting the front axle forward on an extended frame— makes the truck extremely stable while jumping cars.

The West of the Story

Unnamed & Untamed is owned by Michael and Judy West of Portland, Oregon and is driven by Terry Woodcock. It most often performs in the West and Northwest.

Its 472-cubic-inch Chevy engine is naturally aspirated with two Predator racing carburetors on gasoline. Horsepower is fed through a turbo 400 transmission custom modified for racing, then through a hand-built chain-drive transfer case that is overdriven 1.5:1.

Unnamed & Untamed is built from a 1942 Dodge Power Wagon body! This truck may not have a name but it has one of the longest wheelbases of any monster truck: 150 inches. This beast is very stable and can jump cars at up to 60 mph!

Power is then routed through two custom-built drive shafts into axles from a Clark 25-ton crane. Both axles steer and have a 18.5:1 gear ratio. The horsepower is put to the ground by the 66-inch-tall Goodyear Terra tires, which weigh 960 pounds apiece!

Another innovation that gives the Unnamed & Untamed truck great stability is the use of airbags as a suspension system. These are heavy rubber bags mounted between the axles and frame. They absorb much of the shock, and cushion the monster's ride. The handling is further controlled through the use of 22 shock absorbers and coil-over springs.

A Real Ground-Hugger

The truck is able to keep its exceptional stability not only through the use of the airbag suspension and long wheelbase, but through the low, ground-hugging profile of the truck.

The beast with no name is one of the "shortest" monsters around. It stands only ten-and-a-half feet high, a full foot or more shorter than most monsters. But it is wide—measuring 12 feet across. Consequently, it is very stable and can jump cars at up to 60 mph!

PONY EXPRESS!

REWRITING THE LEGEND!

Legends come and legends go, but some legends live for centuries! This is the case with Tommy Bryant's Pony Express! Owner/operator Bryant has taken the theme of the original Pony Express of the Old West—reliability, shrewdness, and just enough unpredictability to keep things interesting—and he has updated it, '90s style! The result is a 700-horsepower (with a 350-horsepower nitrous kit for a total of more than 1000 horsepower) metal-munching machine that is second to none!

Based out of *Avalon Beach, Florida*, Bryant used his salvage yard in Pensacola as the launching ground for Pony Express. A 1967 Ford Mustang body helps give Pony Express its good ol' American red, white and blue appeal.

MONSTER FACTS

Name: Pony Express
Body: 1967 Ford Mustang Fastback with hydraulic tilt front end
Engine: 528-cubic-inch Ford
Frame: Eight-inch by three-inch by one-quarter-inch steel boxed
Height: 12 feet
Interior: Custom red velour
Lights: 11 KC Daylighters
Shocks: Five-ton Military (12 in all)
Springs: Five-ton Military
Steering: Front and rear
Tires: 66- by 43-inch Goodyear Terra
Transfer Case: 205 Ford
Transmission: C-6 Ford Automatic
Weight: 15,000 pounds
Width: 12 feet, 2 inches

Pony Express does a header!

Pony has been thrilling fan at shows and fairs for years! Along with car-crushing, Pony Express pulls the sled and runs the mud bog with the best of them. Pony Express has been showing off down Texas way as of late, but has toured all over the United States and Canada.

CASPER!

CATCH THE SPIRIT!

Throw away those notions that Casper is a friendly ghost. While Casper has sent many a wreck to an early auto graveyard, this "ghostmaker" is downright mean!

Casper was built and designed by Dale and Cheryl Harris, out of Pearl, Mississippi. Casper is a refurbished 1980 Toyota. It stands 13 feet tall and 12½ feet wide and it weighs 18,000 pounds.

The frame is tubed and hand-made, with polished diamond-check aluminum. Casper gets its muscle from a Chevy-powered 454, pumping 1,200 horsepower with two 1150 Holly dominator carburetors.

Add a turbo 400 transmission, a two-and-a-half-ton transfer

Photo © Starlog Communications International, Inc., by Scott W. Aszkenas.

Dale Harris of Pearl, Mississippi stands beside his pride and joy.
This not-so-friendly ghost stands 13 feet tall and 12½ feet wide and weighs 18,000 pounds.

Casper gets its muscle from a Chevy powered 454, pumping 1,200 horsepower with two 1150 Holly dominator carburetors.

Casper isn't afraid of puny fire!

Photo © Starlog Communications International, Inc., by Scott W. Aszkenas.

Casper is a refurbished 1980 Toyota. Go get 'em, Casper!

case with 15-ton Clark planetary four-wheel steering axles, and Firestone terra tires mounted on white modular steel wheels measuring 73 by 44 by 32 inches, and you've got a real four-wheel metal monster!

For suspension, Casper has got a custom six-leaf spring and 12 Monroe magnum gas 80 shock absorbers. For protection, Casper uses a four-leg, four-loop, .095 tubing roll bar, custom built by Kirk Racing products.

Casper was on tour recently in Puerto Rico for two months. During that tour, Casper finished in third place against ten other monster trucks. It would've done even better except for a flat tire, but those are the breaks!

Casper has torn it up with TNT Motor Sports and Agri Shows, making competition runs with 12 to 15 other monster trucks throughout the United States. Casper is sponsored in part by Cherry Picker Parts of Sorrento, Louisiana.

Casper was on tour recently in Puerto Rico for two months. During that tour, Casper finished in third place against ten other monster trucks.

CLYDESDALE!

THE KING OF CHEVYS!

When you hear the word "Clydesdale" you think of the huge horses that pull a beer wagon. Well, this monster truck, the Clydesdale, lives up to the image of that massive, powerful horse.

It may not haul around the King of Beers—but it does lay a serious claim to being King of the Chevys. It's the creation of Bennett Clark of Canton, Georgia, who has been racing it for years and has made an impressive showing in every race he has ever entered.

Clark first got into motorsports through bogging—running big-tired trucks through the heavy, slippery red muck of Georgia. Then he built a customized pickup show truck that he displayed at local car shows and custom car shows.

Clark's show trucks grew larger and larger, as he added even bigger engines and more chrome to beautify his beasts. Finally, he ended up with the truck you see here, a beautifully finished and painted truck that's powerful enough for racing on the national level.

The truck is based on a Chevy 3500 pickup. It has been extensively rebuilt to meet the tough standards of monster-truck racing, both in the frame and drivetrain sections.

The frame, for example, is a box-tube frame with a national stock-car roll cage for safety. It was modified so that the front axle is moved a little forward, giving the truck a 144½-inch wheelbase.

The engine is a 542-cubic-inch Chevy that develops about 1,200 horsepower. This is linked up to a turbo 400 transmission, Rockwell transfer case, and international axles.

That powerplant is mounted back three feet in the truck, putting about half of it in the cab—as you might find in a van. This gives the truck better balance so it's easier to handle on both straight ahead races and obstacle course competitions.

Clydesdale leaps over the junkers during a race against King Krunch.

BLAZE OF GLORY!

MISSISSIPPI BLAZER!

Blaze of Glory was the first monster Blazer ever built. It is the creation of Bubba and Melanie Starnes, who wanted to get into the fun and excitement of monster-truck racing.

Since that time, the truck has taken them all over the coun-try, to many monster truck events, country fairs, and custom car shows. At country fairs they give rides to children. Blaze of Glory is so big it can carry 30 kids at one time!

This truck was virtually hand-built by Bubba, who con-

Before Blaze of Glory was built, no one had ever
converted a Blazer into a monster truck before. Blaze of Glory has a
big block Chevy 454 engine, fed by a 830 cfm Holley carburetor, racing quality, and a tunnel ram.

This truck was virtually hand-built by owner Bubba Starnes, who converted a 1977 Chevy Blazer to monster-truck size by first building up the frame. The beautiful paint job on the body was done by Richard Starnes, with the artwork finished by Leon Hemphill, who painted a beautiful "Blaze of Glory" theme on the sides of the truck.

verted a 1977 Chevy Blazer to monster-truck size by first building up the frame.

The frame is custom made of 4x4 square tubing, installed under and welded to the stock Chevy Blazer frame. The design, fabrication, and welding was done by Bubba.

The suspension was carefully designed and crafted to fit under the truck. This was made of leaf springs, coil springs, and shock absorbers. There are also traction bars up front, with two hydraulic cylinders (one in each bar) to provide stability and shock-absorbing action when Blaze of Glory rams into cars!

Then Bubba had to decide how to power this monster. He used a big block Chevy 454 engine, fed by a 830 cfm Holley carburetor, racing quality, and a tunnel ram.

The tunnel ram is used because it more effectively routes the air-fuel mixture to the eight cylinders. This setup allows the engine to put out about 600 honest horsepower.

The 600 horses are then fed through a turbo 400 automatic transmission, then a two-and-a-half-ton military transfer case. The transfer case routes the power to the front and rear driveshafts. These driveshafts run into the two five-ton Rockwell military axles with 15-ton Clark planetary gears in the ends.

The truck weighs 16,000 pounds, which is heavy by today's race-truck standards. But the truck is amazingly agile, and can easily take flight after bouncing off a pile of cars!

The interior was kept basically stock, with the exception of special racing running gear such as two racing seats and Auto Meter gauges.

The truck weighs 16,000 pounds, which is heavy by today's race-truck standards. But the truck is amazingly agile, and can easily take flight into the air after bouncing off a pile of cars!

Bubba and Melanie would like to thank Tony Neal for his help with the truck.

GONE AWOL

OVER THE HILL ... ANY HILL!

Back in the Spring of 1980, Gone AWOL was just a gleam in Gene Fannie Jr.'s eye. "It took me two-and-a-half years to build it, and another five years of fine tuning," says Fannie, who is from Derry, Pennsylvania.

But there was no doubt, from the moment the last bolt was tightened, that this monster was destined for greatness. Sure enough, the first time Gone AWOL ever entered a competition (a tractor pull in New York City's famed Madison Square Garden, no less,) it won two first prizes.

"We wanted our vehicle to be a little different," says Fannie. "We went heavy with the chrome so it stands out more."

Why is it called Gone AWOL?

"The name really fits," Fannie responds. "We started with an M715 Kaiser Jeep, and about the only thing left is the canvas top. There's not too much left that is original Army.

The rest of the jeep has gone AWOL. For those of you who may not be familiar with the military terminology, AWOL stands for Away Without Leave."

How does Fannie feel when audiences roar for his truck?

"Makes me feel good," he says. "Most of the other trucks are Fords or Chevys. They like seeing an Army truck."

So, how do you improve on such an awesome collection of gears and wheels?

"Well," Fannie says, rubbing his jaw, "we've got a Chevrolet 512 motor now, built by the Urchek Brothers of Blairsville, Pennsylvania—but one day we hope to make it a 572- to 600-inch engine."

When this happens, watch for Gone AWOL to come back over the hill, chewing up the competition like a tough drill sergeant working on a new recruit!

Gone *AWOL* won two first prizes the first time it ever competed!

Gone AWOL's wheels pick up the mud and throw it!

Gene Fannie Jr. at work on his pride and joy

TERMINATOR!

HASTA LA VISTA, BABY!

Look out, Arnold Schwarzenegger! Judgment day is here, and you're not the only Terminator in town anymore.

The Terminator monster truck is based on a 1979 Ford Bronco XLT. This 13-foot tall, 13,000-pound monster was built by Jerry Richmond of Ashtabula, Ohio, who also drives the truck at shows.

Terminator is powered by a 1975 460-cubic-inch big-block Ford, bored .030 over, balanced and blueprinted. The 460 also has TRW 12.1 to 1 pistons and Compettition Cams cam and valve train.

The fuel comes through a single Predator carburetor mounted on a Edelbrock intake. The headers are custom built by the owner. The transmission was built by Quality Transmission of Kingsville, Ohio.

The frame is stock with a custom-built subframe. The truck rides on custom-built 15-leaf, 28-inch arch springs. The hard landings that this beast faces each time it leaps into the air are handled by 20 Rugged Trail shocks.

Traction is provided by 66-inch-tall Firestone terras mounted on 25- by 36-inch steel wheels from FTC Wheels of Franceville, Indiana. Five-ton axles have been mated with 20-ton Clark planetaries. Power is divided by a two-and-a-half-ton air-shift transfer case.

Other special features on the Terminator include: a tilt front end, rear wheel steering, a warn winch front bumper, a Fey Wrangler rear bumper, a stainless light bar with six Baja lasar lights, custom chrome lettering and custom pinstriping, a triple tube roll bar and more.

The Terminator has appeared on the ESPN cable television network, as well as in *Four Wheel & Off Road* and *Pulling Power* magazines.

Terminator is based on a 1979 Ford Bronco XLT and is powered by a 460 big-block Ford engine!

VIRGINIA GIANT!

DON'T MESS WITH THE VIRGINIA GIANT

Ever heard of the Virginia Giant? No, it's not a new baseball team—it's a monster of a monster truck, and it's mean! Diehl Wilson, operating out of Winchester, Virginia, took a year to put together this awesome demolition machine. Asked what the Virginia Giant specializes in, Diehl replies, "Crushing just about anything that gets in its way."

Utilizing a F250 Ford
three-quarter-ton frame, Rockwell military
centers, and topped off with a standard Ford body, the 429 NASCAR engine
generates enough muscle for this 13,000 lb. beast to move at speeds up to 40 mph, and the pulling power to
move 60,000 lbs. So, what do you get for $150,000 worth of truck? "Well," says Diehl, "we do real well in competition, in obstacle
course races, crushing cars, barreling through mud holes, pulling sleds. Plus, our truck looks a little fancier, and people seem to
appreciate that. One fact folks appreciate for sure—if the Virginia Giant is coming—get out of the way!" says Diehl.

MODERN DAY OUTLAW!

BUSTER GUFFY'S ARKANSAS MONSTER!

Modern Day Outlaw hails from Griffithville, Arkansas, a town that, according to owner Buster Guffy, has a population of 254 people and one monster truck! The truck wasn't always from Arkansas, however. This is a truck with a story.

Guffy originally built the truck in the late 1980s when he was living in Coconut Creek, Florida. After eight months of hard work and tens of thousands of dollars spent on high-performance parts and special heavy-duty truck parts, Guffy hit the road, heading for Motown—Detroit, Michigan—for his first show

As luck would have it, he hit a patch of ice on the highway. The trailer and the truck slid sideways and then flipped over. The monster was not a total loss: Guffy was able to fix it overnight and still won three of the five monster truck races he competed in that weekend.

Depressed but not broken, Guffy towed the truck home for a total rehab. After another three months of hard work and loads of money, he rebuilt the truck and gave it its current S10 body.

Right after that, Guffy moved to Arkansas.

Standout in Customization

The truck has a number of fine customized features that make it a standout. The body paint features a silver base highlighted with gold, blue, and red/purple stripes, done by Oxidines Auto Body of Cahokia, Illinois.

Modern Day Outlaw has a hydraulic dump bed, tilting hood, House of Steel triple roll bar, twelve KC stainless-steel lights,

The Outlaw weighs 10,900 pounds and is light enough to fly over cars, but heavy enough to flatten them when it lands.

and a full diamond aluminum bed, with bed rails and custom grille by Dee Zee of Des Moines, Iowa.

The interior has a stock dashboard, but just about everything else inside the cabin has been customized. This includes custom seats, full inside roll cage built by Classic Dynamics, fire extinguisher, kill switches and Simpson seat belts.

The truck is powered by a Chevy 496-cubic-inch marine block, fed by two Predator carbs, producing about 750 horsepower. The transmission is an Allison AT-540, hooked up to a two-and-a-half-ton air-shift military transfer case.

The axles are five-ton Rockwells, with custom-made springs and 16 Trailmaster N7 gas shocks. The huge 66-inch-tall Goodyear Terra tires are mounted on 25-inch-deep steel wheels, giving the Outlaw a total height of ten feet, seven inches. The Outlaw weighs 10,900 pounds.

Guffy continues to tour with Modern Day Outlaw. They continue to leap and crush—from coast to coast!

Photo © Starlog Communications International, Inc., by Scott W. Aszkenas.

BIGTOW

BY HOOK OR CROOK THIS ONE'S A WINNER!

Bigtow pops a wheelie during a show in Fort Worth, Texas!

Bigtow has a functioning hook—so it can crush cars while hauling your car away at the same time.

Bigtow's Ford 460 V8 powerplant produces 900 horsepower.

MONSTER FACTS

Name: Bigtow
Builder: Ray Piorkowski
Engine: Ford 460 V8
Horsepower: 900
Displacement: 500 cubic inches
Pistons: TRW forged aluminum
Intake: Don Hampton 671 Blower
Camshaft: Cam Dynamics
Carburetors: Predator
Air Cleaners: Mr. Gasket
Headers: Headmann
Transmission: C-6 Auto
Transmission built by: Accurate Transmission
Transfer Case: Two-and-a-half-ton military
Front & Rear End: Five-ton military with
Rockwell Planetaries
Driveshafts: Custom-made ¼-inch thick tubes
Frame: Ford one-ton highly modified
Wheelbase: 133 inches
Front suspension: Ten leafs custom—St. Louis Springs
Shocks: Ranco
Traction Bars: Custom Hydraulic
Steering: Hydraulic
Fuel Tank: 20-gallon custom
Ground Clearance: 24 inches
Weight: 19,500 pounds
Tires: 66- by 43- by 25-inch Goodyear Terra
Wheels: 36- by 25-inch modular steel
Body type: 1979 Ford
Paint: Acrylic Enamel, Bright red
Stripes: Allen's Striping
Front End: Hydraulic tilt

Bigtow kicks Lethal *Weapon*'s butt during a race at the Pontiac Silverdome in Pontiac, Michigan.

A NIGHT AT THE RACES!

1994 USHRA ACTION!

Enough specifications, already—let's get down to some action! The Nassau County Coliseum in Uniondale, New York is jam-packed with roaring fans and the monsters are ready to rumble.

The monster trucks in this event, held under the auspices of the United States Hot Rod Association (USHRA), race in what is called the "Roundy-Round" fashion.

The indoor arena, big enough for a hockey game, is relatively small when compared to the beasts, so tight turns are in order when racing—and that demands expert driving since these trucks steer both in the front and in the rear.

The trucks start on opposite sides of the arena, pointing in opposite directions. Exactly twenty feet in front of each truck is a row of junkers. With the starter's signal, the thunderous roar of mutated powerplants fill the arena. The trucks go around each turn at the end of the arena once—referred to as the "near turn" and the "far turn"—and finish after leaping over and crushing their first row of cars a second time.

Photo © Starlog Communications International, Inc., by Scott W. Aszkenas.

Round One

The first race of the evening results in Bob Fisher's UFO getting a very slow start, allowing an easy victory to Dennis Anderson's Gravedigger.

Carolina Crusher—driven by Gary Porter, a 31-year-old from Wadesboro, North Carolina, one of the few drivers on the circuit who travels alone—had an easy victory in the second match when Paul Shafer's Monster Patrol came down hard on the left front tire after leaping a set of cars, tearing out the suspension.

Allen Pezo, a 25-year-old from Michigan, drove the Predator truck to victory over Kirk Dabner's Nitemare. An early puff of smoke from Predator didn't develop into the expected trouble, and the win was easy after Nitemare spun out in the far turn.

Mike Wales' Liquidator, the only non-supercharged monster in the field, struggled throughout the race with rear-steering problems, but won nonetheless when David Morris in Equalizer spun in the far turn.

In the last match of the first round, Fred Shafer, a veteran of 15 years behind the wheel of a beast, drove Bear Foot to a dominant victory over Wayne Smozaner's Tropical Thunder. The winners plus the top three fastest losers moved into the second round.

All else equal, the truck that leaps the most cars wins the race. It's faster to fly than it is to drive.

The AM/PM Rocket! Lift off! AM/PM Rocket wants to get across as much of the row as possible before those front wheels come down.

Photo © Starlog Communications International, Inc., by Scott W. Aszkenas.

Round Two

The second round began with an equal-matched pairing as only Fred Shafer's perfect driving line allowed Bear Foot to defeat Gravedigger. The race was without incident and the margin of victory was .47 second.

Carolina Crusher cruised to its second easy victory of the evening when, with a huge puff of smoke, Predator blew a $30,000 engine at the beginning of the race.

Equalizer beat Tropical Thunder when Wayne Smozaner misjudged the first turn and never recovered. After the race, Equalizer developed mechanical problems of its own and had to be replaced in the semi-finals by Gravedigger.

Liquidator—as always, out-powered by its opponent, lost a squeaker to UFO

closest monster truck race of all time. It was the 10,050-pound Bear Foot, with its Dodge engine and body, versus the five-ton-even Carolina Crusher, wearing a Chevy body and powered by a Rodeck 557 engine. Bear Foot sported 1500 horsepower, while the Crusher boasted 1400. Maybe it was the extra hundred horses that led Bear Foot to a seemingly impossible .06 second victory.

In the finals, Gravedigger came away with all the marbles when Carolina Crusher got out of shape and lost time in the far turn. The winner, ironically, was a truck that wouldn't have made it into the semi-finals if Equalizer hadn't developed mechanical difficulties.

Leaving the arena, folks were a little light-headed with excitement (and with the ringing in their ears.) Everyone knew they had gotten their money's worth!

Semis, Final

In a rematch of their Round One challenge, the semi-finals began with Gravedigger using its power advantage to defeat UFO. Gravedigger is a 10,000-pound truck with a Chevrolet body and a Chevy Bow-Tie block engine, producing 1435 horsepower. UFO, on the other hand, is heavier, weighing 10,500 pounds, and—with a Ford body and engine—produces only 900 horsepower.

The second semi-final match was the closest race of the night, and possibly the

For safety reasons, trucks no longer race side by side, as these do.

Photo © Starlog Communications International, Inc., by Scott W. Aszkenas.

Bigfoot 4x4x4 is all gassed up and ready to go!

Rollin' Thunder, a monster van, crushes with the best of them!

Big Brutus has six big wheels to crush with!

Stomper takes a nasty tumble

3428

INDEX